CAT JOKE BOOK

To Mor

from Liz

What do you call the cat that was caught by the police?

The purrpatrator

What does a cat have that no other animal has?

Kittens

What did the cat say when the mouse got away?

You've got to be kitten me!

Why don't cats play poker in the jungle?

There are too many cheetahs

Why was the cat sitting on the computer?

To keep an eye on the mouse

Why did the cat wear a dress?

She was feline fine

What did the cat say when he lost all his money?
I'm paw!

Why don't cats like online shopping?
They prefer a cat-alogue

What do you call a pile of kittens?
A meowntain

What is a cat's favorite song?
Three Blind Mice

What do you call a cat that lives in an igloo?
An eskimew!

What do cats like to eat for breakfast?
Mice Krispies

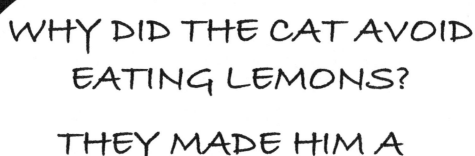

What's worse than raining cats and dogs?

Hailing taxis

What's the worst kind of cat?

A cat-astrophe

What do you call a cat in a station wagon?

A car-pet

What do you call at cat that goes bowling?

An alley cat

Why was the cat disqualified from the game?

It was a cheetah

Why did the cat run away from the tree?

It was scared of its bark

What would a cat say if you stepped on its tail?
"Me-OW!"

What did the alien say to the cat?
"Take me to your litter"

What is a cat's favorite color?
Purrrple

What's a cat's favorite dessert?
A mice cream cone

How do cats get over a fight?
They hiss and make up

What did the gym coach say to the cat?
Have you paid your annual fleas?

What does the narcissistic cat say as she looks in the mirror?

I am pawsitively gorgeous

What do you get if you cross a cat with a bottle of vinegar?

A sourpuss!

What do cats wear at night?

Paw-jamas

What do you call a cat with eight legs that likes to swim?

An octo-puss

Why did the cat join the Red Cross?

She wanted to be a first-aid kit!

Why are you so upset that I shed on the couch?

It's called fur-niture!

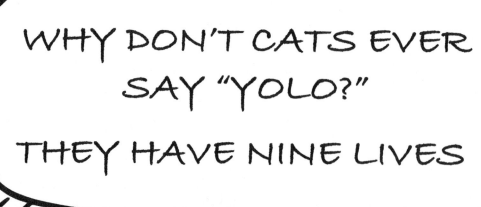

What do you call a sad cat that's in a hurry?

A Russian Blue

Which two sodas does a cat like best?

Dr. Peppurr and Meowntain Mew

What do you call it when a swarm of cats slows down your airplane? **Purr-bulence**

What do you call it when a cat wins first place at a dog show? **A cat-has-trophy**

What's a British cat's favorite fantasy book?

Hairy Pawter and the Philoso-purr's Stone

What do you call a kitten that cuts her hair really short?

A bob cat!

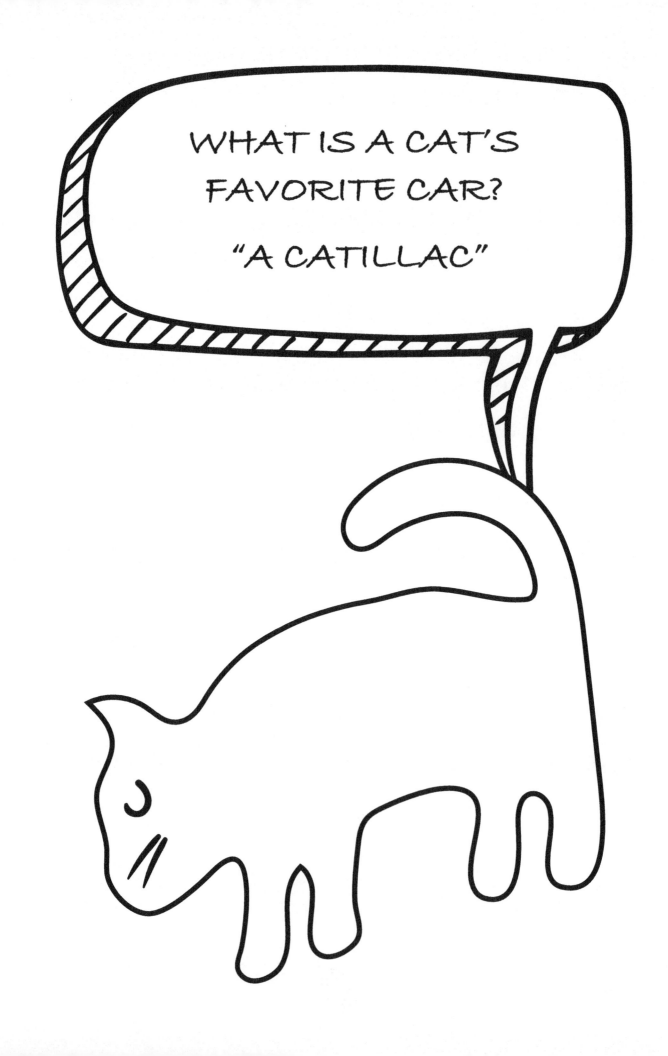

What did the cat do after her home was broken into?

She called claw enforcement

What's a tomcat's ultimate romantic goal?

To find a nice girl cat and whisker away

Why don't cats mind when someone copies them?

Because imitation is the sincerest form of cattery

What's a cat's favorite Shakespeare play?

Romeow and Mew-liet

What do you call a cat sleeping in your shoe?

Puss in boots

What did the cat say when his friend asked if he was lying?

I'm not kitten you

"WHAT HAPPENED TO YOUR CAT? HE WAS RUNNING AROUND THE WHOLE VILLAGE LIKE THE DEVIL WAS ON HIS TAIL."

"WELL HE GOT CASTRATED YESTERDAY AND NOW HE'S CANCELING ALL HIS DATES."

Is he catatonic?
No, just taking a cat nap

What do you call a big pile of cats?
A purramid

What kind of sports car does a cat drive?
A Furrari

What do you call a cat that's a beauty influencer?
Glamourpuss

What do you get if you cross a cat with Father Christmas?
Santa Claws!

Where does a cat go when it loses its tail?
The re-tail store!

"YOUR CAT KILLED MY PITBULL."
-
"NO WAY, THAT IS IMPOSSIBLE."
-
"YES, HE CHOKED ON HER."

What do you call a cat who loves to bowl?
An alley cat!

What do cats love to do in the morning?
Read the mewspaper

What do baby cats always wear?
Diapurrs!

What's another name for a cat's house?
A scratch pad

What should you say to your cat when you leave the house?
"Have a mice day!"

Where do cats always fly out of when they travel?
Kitty Hawk

HOW DID THE CAT GET THE FIRST PRIZE AT A BIRD SHOW?

SOMEBODY DIDN'T SHUT THE CHAMPION'S CAGE PROPERLY.

How does a cat sing scales?
Do-re-mew!

What's a cat's favorite subject in school?
Hisss-tory

What types of cats purr the best?
Purrr-sians

What sports do cats play?
Hairball

How do you make a cat happy?
Send it to the Canary Islands!

Why do you have to be careful when it rains cats and dogs?
Don't step in a poodle!

"OUR CAT WAS STUPID ENOUGH TO DRINK SOME GASOLINE YESTERDAY. SHE SPENT TWO HOURS RACING THROUGH THE FLAT, THEN JUST FLOPPED ON HER BACK AND WAS TOTALLY STILL. "

-

"OH NO, IS SHE DEAD?"

-

"NO, JUST RAN OUT OF GAS"

What do you call a dishonest African cat?

A "lyin' cub"

Why was the cat so small?

It ate only condensed milk

Where do cats write down their notes?

On scratch paper!

What do you call a cat that gives up?

A "quitty"

What does a mouse weigh on a cat's scale?

About three pounces

What happened to the cat that ate the ball of yarn?

It had mittens!

IN THE MIDDLE OF THE DESERT ONE CAT SAYS TO THE OTHER,

-

"OH BOY, I HAVE TO PEE SO BADLY."

-

"WHY DON'T YOU JUST DO IT?"

-

"I CAN'T. THERE IS NO LITTER BOX."

Why are cats good at video games?
Because they have nine lives!

Why did the cats ask for a drum set?
They wanted to make some mewsic!

How did the Mom Cat know she was pregnant?
Her test was pawsitive

What normally happens when kitties go on a first date?
They hiss

When cats need to go to the airport, who do they call?
A tabby

Why did the cat have to go to an accountant?
They got caught up in a purramid scheme

WHEN YOU ARRIVE HOME AFTER WORK, YOUR DOG WILL BE EXTREMELY HAPPY TO SEE YOU AND WILL LICK YOUR FACE.

THE CAT WILL STILL BE MAD AT YOU FOR LEAVING IN THE FIRST PLACE.

What made the cat upgrade his phone?

He wanted to finally get pawtrait mode

Why are kittens actually excellent bosses?

They have great littership

Before going after a mouse, what did the dad cat say to his family? **"Let us prey"**

What did the kitten have at their birthday party?

A pounce house

What do you call it when a cat is super-stylish?

"Haute-cat-ture"

Why did the kitty get an "A" on their English assignment?

They properly used an independent claws

KNOCK KNOCK

WHO'S THERE?

CAT! CAT WHO?

"CAT ME OUTSIDE, HOW BOUT
DAT?!"

When a cat doesn't want to say goodbye, what do they say instead? **"See ya litter!"**

Why don't you want to play Monopoly with a cat?
They tend to be cheetahs

Before a cat fight, what is usually said?
"Hold my purrse"

What do cats quote from the movie Bridesmaids?
"Help me, I'm paw!"

Why was the teenage cat sent to his room?
He was in a bad meowd

What did one cat say while her friend was complaining?
"Tail me about it"

A CATS TO-DO LIST:

EAT

SLEEP

FREAK OUT IN THE MIDDLE OF THE
NIGHT

Why are cats bad at making decisions?

They become so purrplexed

How did one cat break up with another?
She said, "We're hisstory!"

Which day of the week do cats love the most?
Caturday

Why do cats make horrible DJs?
They always paws the tunes

What did the mom and dad cat say about their wedding day? **"It was unfurrgetable!"**

How did the cat comic know he was funny?
The audience was meow-ling with laughter

DOGS HAVE OWNERS CATS HAVE STAFF

Why was the animal lover so untrustworthy?
She kept letting the cat out of the bag!

What did the sick cat say?
"I feel clawful!"

Why did some cat friends go to the mall?
There was a buy-one-get-one-furry deal

What's a kitten's favorite kind of sticker?
Scratch and sniff

Did you hear about the cat that climbed the Himalayas?
She was a sher-paw

Who was the most powerful cat in China?
Chairman Miaow

IF CATS
COULD
TEXT YOU
BACK,
THEY
WOULDN'T

What is smarter than a talking cat?
A spelling bee!

What do you get when you cross a chick with an alley cat?
A peeping tom

Did you hear about the cat who drank five bowls of water?
He set a new lap record

What do you get if you cross a tiger with a snowman?
Frostbite!

Why do cats make terrible storytellers?
They only have one tail

My cat told a joke today but I didn't laugh.
He took it purr-sondal

DON'T
TELL ME
WHAT TO
DO, YOU
ARE NOT
MY CAT

Someone made a joke about my three-legged cat.
Major faux paw

What do you get if you cross a cat with a parrot?
A carrot

Where did the school kittens go on their field trip?
To the mewseum

What do you call a cat that wakes up with an alarm clock?
Catsup

Why do cats like to eat fur balls?
They love a good gag!

What is it called when a cat stops?
Paws

CAT PUNS
FREAK
MEOWT.
SERIOUSLY
I'M NOT
KITTEN

Why did the mother cat put stamps on her kittens?
She wanted to mail a litter!

What do cats have minty breath?
They use mousewash!

What would you drink at the mad Catter's tea party?
Kit-tea!

When is it bad luck to see a black cat?
When you're a mouse

What do you call a flying cat?
I'm-paws-sible

What do you call an animal that can jump higher than a kangaroo? **Cathletic**

CAT IS
ALWAYS
ON THE
WRONG
SIDE OF
THE DOOR

Who are cats going to vote for in November?
Hillary Kitten

Why shouldn't you kidnap the kitten, Keanu?
Because curiousity killed the cat burglar

What do you get if you cross a cat with a dark horse?
Kitty Perry

Why did the cat sleep under the car?
Because he wanted to wake up oily

What do you feed an invisible cat?
Evaporated milk

What do you call a cat race?
A meowathon

CATS SPEND
HALF THEIR
LIFE ASLEEP
AND HALF
MAKING
VIRAL VIDEOS

What is a cats favorite vegetable?

As-purr-agus

Did you know that cats designed the great pyramids of Giza? **It was all drawn out on paw-pyrus**

What do cats wear at night?

Paw-jamas

What do you call a cat on ice?

One cool cat

What do you call a cat that does tricks?

A magic kit

What's the first thing you say to a cat?

HELLO KITTY!

DOGS CANT

OPERATE

MRI

SCANNERS

BUT

CATSCAN

What do you need to get a fast cat to use the litter box?
Quicksand

How do you make cats furry?
The spin cycle

Why did the cat cross the road?
It was the chicken's day off!

What do you call it when a cat is getting old?
GrandPAW

What is a cat tantrum?
A Hissy Fit

What looks like half a cat?
The other half

NEVER FEED
YOUR CAT
ANYTHING
THAT
CLASHES
WITH THE
CARPET

What kind of cat works in a hospital?

A first aid kitten

How is a cat like a coin?

It has a head on one side and a tail on the other

Why can't cats play go fish with each other?

They get too distracted by the fish

What does a cat do after it wakes up in the morning?

It goes back to sleep

What do you get if you cross a leopard with a watchdog?

A terrified postman

How do you pet a psychopaths cat?

You get it out of the microwave

BATHING CATS IS A MARTIAL ART

How do you know cat's don't always land on their feet?
Mufasa

What does a cat drink when it's depressed?
Whiskey

What is it called when a cat wins a dog show?
A CAT-HAS-TROPHY!

Why are there no cats on Mars?
Curiosity killed them all

My cat made an onlyfans account
People love her cat-nips!

I started blogging by writing about all the best things about cats **It was my cat-A-list**

IF YOU
DON'T TALK
ABOUT YOUR
CATNIP
WHO
WILL?

What's a Russian cats favorite book to read?

The Communist Meownifesto

Schrodinger's Cat recently went on a crime spree

He's wanted dead and alive

Two cat's are on a roof, which one falls off first?

The one with the smallest mu

When women get to a certain age, they start collecting cats..

This is known as the many paws

What did the cat like most about the iPod?

The pawsability

When do cats beg for food?

Every tuna half hours

CAT
THOUGHTS MY
HUMAN
RARELY EVER
LICKS
HIMSELF
THATS NASTY
BRUH

How does a cat make bread?

From scratch

Never say anything offensive to Cats.

You might hurt their Felines

Why are cats afraid of space?

Because it's a vacuum

Did you know that all cats are Jewish?

Their surname it Katz afterall

I used to work at a cats home , but I had to leave.

They reduced meowers

Why was the cat laying on the globe?

He wanted to take a cat map

LETTING THE
CAT OUT
OF
THE BAG IS
EASIER
THAN
PUTTING IT
BACK IN

I had been told that the training procedure with cats was difficult. It's not. **Mine had me trained in two days**

What do you call a peeping Tom-Cat?
A purrrvert

What does a cat need to drive a car?
A purrmit

What do you smell if you (accidentally) burn a cat?
Purr-fume

I think my cat might be a communist
He won't shut up about Mao

Did you hear about the time a cat got into a mousehole?
Casualties were **cat**astrophic

CATS ARE
BUILT
TO ALLOW THE
HUMAN VOICE
TO GO IN
ONE
EAR AND OUT
THE OTHER

What word do millennial cats overuse?
Litter-ally

Why was the cat nervous to debate?
He had a furmidable opponent!

Someone made a joke about my three-legged cat.
Major faux paw

Do you think your cat would enjoy these cat puns?
Purrhaps!

Did you hear about the cat who drank 5 bowls of water?
They set a new lap record

My cat got stolen.
I think she was taken by a purr snatcher

PETTING
A
CAT
WILL
LEAVE
YOU
FELINE
GOOD

LIVE
LONG
AND
PAWSPER

WATCH ME

SNIP

NOW

WATCH ME

SPAY

SPAY

THERE ARE MANY REASONS TO ADOPT A CAT. BUT ALL YOU NEED IS ONE

IF SLEEPING
WAS AN
OLYMPIC
SPORT,
MY
CAT WOULD
WIN THE
GOLD

Number Cats

There were two cats
1 of their names was one two three
The other name was une duex triois
They had a race across the lake, which one won?
One two three won, because une duex trois cat sank

Movies

A man in a movie theater notices what looks like a cat sitting next to him. "Are you a cat?" asked the man, surprised. "Yes." "What are you doing at the movies?" The cat replied, "Well, I liked the book."

Front Seat

A policeman in the big city stops a man in a car with a Siberian Lynx in the front seat. "What are you doing with that Siberian Lynx?" He exclaimed, "You should take it to the zoo." The following week, the same policeman sees the same man with the cat again in the front seat, with both of them wearing sunglasses. The policeman pulls him over. "I thought you were going to take that cat to the zoo!" The man replied, "I did. We had such a good time we are going to the beach this weekend!"

Dispatch

The police dispatch picks up the phone and writes down the call for help: "Please send someone urgent, a cat has broken in!" The police dispatcher responded, "Sir, I don't think I heard you correctly? A cat at your home?" "A cat! He has invaded my house and is walking towards me! Again the police dispatch tried to correct him "But how so? You mean a thief?" "NO! I'm talking about a freaking cat, the one that does 'meow, meow', and it's coming my way!.... You have to come now!" "So what about this cat coming toward you?" the officer replies trying to grasp the situation "He's going to kill me, now he's going mental! And you will be the reason I die" "Who is talking?" the officer asks The parrot, you jac**ss!

Top Ten Reasons Why Dogs Are Better Pets Than Cats

1. Dogs will tilt their heads and try to understand every word you say. Cats will ignore you and take a nap.

2. Cats look silly on a leash.

3. When you come home from work, your dog will be happy and lick your face. Cats will still be mad at you for leaving in the first place.

4. Dogs will give you unconditional love until the day they die. Cats will make you pay for every mistake you've ever made since the day you were born.

5. A dog knows when you're sad. And he'll try to comfort you. Cats don't care how you feel, as long as you remember where the can opener is.

6. Dogs will bring you your slippers. Cats will drop a dead mouse in your slippers.

7. When you take them for a ride, dogs will sit on the seat next to you. Cats have to have their own private basket, or they won't go at all.

8. Dogs will come when you call them. And they'll be happy. Cats will have someone take a message and get back to you.

9. Dogs will play fetch with you all day long. The only thing cats will play with all day long are small rodents or bugs, preferably ones that look like they're in pain.

10. Dogs will wake you up if the house is on fire. Cats will quietly sneak out the back door.

Large Litter

A little boy calls his friend and says: "Help, my cat has given birth to 10 kittens! I do not know where to leave them .... because I do not have enough space at home!" Then the friend replies: "You can leave them in front of some bar or restaurant, there they can find food!". The boy takes his friend's advice but calls him later with the news: "It didn't work, the kittens came right back home!" So his friend says: "That's fine, so leave them in front of the closed shops, where there are no lights and they will not be able to find their way home". The boy does as he said but then calls him: "It didn't work, the cats have returned home as if they had GPS!" And the friend replied annoyed. "at this point go farther than you've ever gone before, turn left, turn right, confuse the hell out of those little buggers." . After about 2 days, the friend calls the boy: "So you got rid of the kittens?" and he replies: "Well let me tell you, I walked for about a day, got lost and I just came back.... if I did not follow the cats I would not have even made it home!".

Printed in Great Britain
by Amazon

75250068R00041